SO-AIZ-120

B.C.—RIGHT ON

by Johnny Hart

FAWCETT GOLD MEDAL • NEW YORK

B.C. RIGHT ON

Copyright © 1967 by Publishers News Syndicate, Inc.

© 1973 CBS Publications, The Consumer Publishing
Division of CBS, Inc. All Rights Reserved

ISBN: 0-449-13645-0

Printed in the United States of America

26   25   24   23   22   21   20   19   18   17

5.2

5.4

hart

5.5

5·6

5·11

BONK

TRUND ·
JUMP JUMP
POUNCE
STOMP
STOMP
POUNCE
JUMP
STOMP

5·18

I **DO** BELIEVE
I HAVE BEEN
PUMMELLED.

hart

5-20

hart

5·22

hart.

WHY DO YOU TAKE IT?
.... WHY DO YOU LAY
THERE AND LET HER
BEAT YOU LIKE THAT?

...WHY DON'T YOU TRY
TO GET AWAY OR
SOMETHING?

5·25

DID YOU EVER TRY TO
SLITHER OFF WITH
FOUR HUNDRED AND
EIGHTY-TWO SLIPPED DISCS?

hart.

pōl·lu'tion *n.*
the result of
polluting.

pōl·lu'ting.
to pollute.

pōl·lute'.
to cause
pollution

5·29

5.30

5-31

6.1

6.2

6·5

6·6

hart

6-7

68

6-13

614

6-15

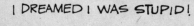

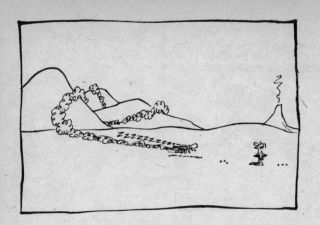

6-24

6-26

6-27

6.28

6·29

PUT YOUR GLASSES
OUT ON THE END
OF YOUR NOSE

6-30

YOUR TOENAILS
COULD USE CUTTING.

hart

7·1

7.3

hart

7-4

hart

7-7

HOW COME, WHEN YOU WALK — YOUR HEELS HIT FIRST, ...

AND WHEN YOU STRUT YOUR TOES HIT FIRST?

7-8

IT SAVES WEAR AND TEAR ON THE OL' ARCHES.

hart

O.K., MEN HERE'S THE BATTING ORDER.

7·11

B.C. LEADS OFF FOLLOWED BY PETER AND CURLS. THOR WILL BAT CLEAN-UP.

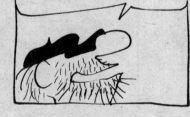

HOW COME I ALWAYS GET THE DIRTY JOBS?

hart

POOK

7-12

YOU JUST 'SHOOK-OFF'
EVERY PITCH YOU'VE GOT!
WHAT THE HECK DO YOU
WANT TO DO?

7.13

BEAN THE UMPIRE.

hart

7.14

TIME! ...LET'S TAKE A LOOK AT THAT BALL!

7-15

COME ON, NOW! .. IT CAN'T BE THAT BIG!

hart

STAR LIGHT STAR BRIGHT, FIRST STAR I SEE TONIGHT.
I WISH I MAY I WISH I MIGHT, HAVE THE WISH I WISH TONIGHT!
7·19
YOU'RE ON, POPS!
hart

7-24

WHOMP

7-26

7-28

SMACK

7-29

nart

8·9

8-11

AN APPLE FOR
YOUR THOUGHTS!

8·14

WILL YOU GET
OUT OF HERE!

hart

8·18

hart

8-21

8-22.

8-23

8.25

9.2

WHY DON'T YOU TELL B.C. HOW YOU FEEL ABOUT HIM?

I CAN'T DO THAT!

BESIDES, ...HE DOESN'T EVEN KNOW I'M ALIVE!

*

9-5

SHE'S ALIVE! ...YOU KLODHOPPER!

hart

9·7

9.11

9.18

9.19

9-20

hart

9·26

CLAP

AAAAAAAHHHHH

THAT'S WHAT
I CALL
EMPATHY!

10-3

hart

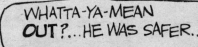

10·6

10-1

10·10

10·11

10·16

1019

10-21

HOLD IT!

LOOK, GROG,... MAKE A DENT IN THE GROUND WITH YOUR HEEL, THEN STAND THE BALL UP! ..IT'S EASIER TO KICK.

10·23

hart

HI THERE, I AM AN APTERYX. A WINGLESS BIRD WITH HAIRY FEATHERS.

10·24

THERE'S SO MUCH TO LEARN......

hart

10·25

hart